REACHING FOR THE STARS

IMAGINE
SPACE

Mike Downs

Rourke
Educational Media

A Division of
Carson
Dellosa
Education

High
Tide

Before Reading: *Building Background Knowledge and Vocabulary*

Building background knowledge can help children process new information and build upon what they already know. Before reading a book, it is important to tap into what children already know about the topic. This will help them develop their vocabulary and increase their reading comprehension.

Questions and Activities to Build Background Knowledge:

1. Look at the front cover of the book and read the title. What do you think this book will be about?
2. What do you already know about this topic?
3. Take a book walk and skim the pages. Look at the table of contents, photographs, captions, and bold words. Did these text features give you any information or predictions about what you will read in this book?

Vocabulary: *Vocabulary Is Key to Reading Comprehension*

Use the following directions to prompt a conversation about each word.

- Read the vocabulary words.
- What comes to mind when you see each word?
- What do you think each word means?

Vocabulary Words:
- astrology
- astronomy
- Milky Way
- satellites
- technology
- UFO

During Reading: *Reading for Meaning and Understanding*

To achieve deep comprehension of a book, children are encouraged to use close reading strategies. During reading, it is important to have children stop and make connections. These connections result in deeper analysis and understanding of a book.

Close Reading a Text

During reading, have children stop and talk about the following:

- Any confusing parts
- Any unknown words
- Text-to-text, text-to-self, text-to-world connections
- The main idea in each chapter or heading

Encourage children to use context clues to determine the meaning of any unknown words. These strategies will help children learn to analyze the text more thoroughly as they read.

When you are finished reading this book, turn to the next-to-last page for **After-Reading Questions** and an **Activity**.

TABLE OF CONTENTS

FIRES IN THE SKY

Ever since people first looked skyward, they've wondered about the cosmos. What were all the lights in the night sky? How did they get there? Before advanced **technology** existed, people could only guess. The Algonquins of North America believed the stars were campfires. The Maori of New Zealand saw some stars as souls of their heroes. The Egyptians thought the **Milky Way** was a heavenly river.

technology (tech-NAH-luh-jee): practical application of knowledge in a particular area

All the stars we see are part of our Milky Way galaxy.

Milky Way (MIL-kee way): This is the galaxy we live in. It has about 100 billion stars. In some places, it looks like a river of lights.

At the same time, some societies noted the predictable movements they saw in the sky. The Babylonians charted the planets and the stars. The Aztecs made accurate calendars that they used for rituals. Almost all societies mixed this type of scientific mapping with religious beliefs. They believed the movement and position of the heavens could predict the future. This is called **astrology**.

astrology (uh-STRAH-luh-jee): using the supposed influence of the stars and planets on human life to predict aspects of future human affairs and terrestrial events

Different societies have different legends for the constellations.

Your Birthday in Outer Space

Many people still believe in astrology. They use the time of day and planets' positions when someone is born to predict what that person will be like.

The ancient Chinese kept **astronomy** and astrology separate. Emperors used the science of astronomy to make calendars. They also had advisors who used astrology to try to predict the future. As math and science advanced, other societies also began to separate the science of astronomy from the religious beliefs of astrology.

Ptolemy was a famous Greek astronomer and mathematician. In about 150 CE (known as the Common Era), he incorrectly determined that Earth was the center of the universe. This belief lasted more than 1,200 years.

astronomy (uh-STRAH-nuh-mee): the study of objects and matter outside Earth's atmosphere, such as the sun, moon, and stars

Saturn

Mars

Neptune

Venus

Sun

Earth

Mercury

Jupiter

Uranus

Earth-centered Solar System

Saturn

Mars

Neptune

Venus

Sun

Earth

Mercury

Jupiter

Uranus

Sun-centered Solar System

As the science of astronomy advanced, mathematicians began to describe the cosmos using numbers and formulas. In the 1500s, Copernicus used math to prove that the sun was the center of our solar system. However, the majority of people, including the Catholic church, still believed Earth was the center of the universe. Copernicus, afraid of the church's response, did not publish his work.

Eventually, science prevailed. Isaac Newton's explanation of gravity explained the orbiting of planets around the sun. Later, Albert Einstein's theory of general relativity explained it even better.

Our Orbiting Home

Today we know we have planets and other objects orbiting around the sun. This means they follow a mostly circular or oval path. The sun is only one star in the Milky Way galaxy, which has more than a hundred billion stars.

Copernicus was a mathematician and an astronomer.

The first recorded invention of the telescope was in 1608. Telescopes allowed astronomers, such as Galileo, to study stars and planets more closely. Maria Mitchell, the first female astronomer in the United States, discovered a comet with a telescope in 1847.

Since then, new telescopes have led to thousands of discoveries. Many new telescopes measure radio waves, microwaves, and other things we can't see. Objects moving away at ultrahigh speeds appear slightly redder. This is called red-shift. With powerful telescopes, astronomers looking at other galaxies can see red-shift. It shows that galaxies are moving apart as the universe expands.

Using a telescope, Galileo discovered the four largest moons around Jupiter. They are sometimes called the Galilean moons.

ROCKET SHIPS AND ALIENS

People have always dreamed of traveling to outer space. But how could explorers ever reach it? Science fiction authors have provided incredible answers over the years. Around 150 CE, the author Lucian wrote about Greek soldiers sailing to the moon. Jules Verne, in 1865, imagined people inside a large, bullet-shaped capsule that shot out of a cannon. In 1928, the German author Thea von Harbou wrote about riding a rocket to the moon.

Astronauts first landed on the moon in 1969.

FROM THE EARTH TO THE MOON

JULES VERNE

As technology gets better, our vision of space is changing. In 1970, Larry Niven wrote the novel *Ringworld*. He imagined a circular space station so big that it stretched around the sun. It was three million times the size of Earth.

Another use of massive space structures appears in the *Halo* game series. Halos are huge, ring-shaped mega-weapons. Each is large enough to stretch around a planet the size of Mars, or about half the size of Earth.

The Force Be with You

The science fiction book *Dune*, by Frank Herbert, introduced the concept of a "Force" long before the *Star Wars* movies arrived. In *Dune*, it was the "Voice," which also included mind control and super-enhanced fighting.

New technology gives us new visions of the future.

In the past, people used their imaginations to visualize space. Early books included simple drawings. In 1902, Georges Méliès made a silent film showing people being shot to the moon inside a large bullet. In the 1960s, television shows such as *Star Trek* used models and camera tricks to make outer space appear exciting. Today, computer-generated imagery (CGI) makes space battles, aliens, and hyperspeed ships look real.

One popular vision of the future includes massive space battleships.

Many popular video games take place in outer space.

Our ideas about aliens have also changed. Many movies today show that alien species might be friendly. That wasn't always the case. In 1953, the movie *War of the Worlds* showed Martians attacking Earth while trying to take over the world. Fifteen years later, *The Green Slime* described an alien goo that transformed into one-eyed, tentacled monsters.

In 1938, Orson Welles broadcasted a live radio program to about 12 million listeners saying that Martians were attacking Earth. It was a fake newscast for entertainment. But, about 1 in 12 people allegedly panicked (some even ran out of their houses!) thinking the story was real and that Earth was under Martian attack!

Some people believe that aliens have already visited Earth in flying saucers or other UFOs. However, the only evidence has been blurry photographs, videos, or personal stories. Many of these incidents have simple explanations. For example, the bright light of the planet Venus is frequently described as a UFO.

UFO (yoo ef oh): acronym that stands for *unidentified flying object*, usually used to refer to possible alien spacecraft

The Roswell Incident

Roswell, New Mexico, is famous for the metallic wreckage of a UFO discovered there in 1947. Citizens were convinced it was an alien spacecraft, but it was actually a crashed military balloon.

THAT'S IMPOSSIBLE!

One thing we didn't imagine was low-Earth orbit becoming a junkyard. We are tracking more than half a million pieces of floating space junk. Most of it is from a satellite blown up in 2007 and two other **satellites** that collided in 2009. The rest includes worn-out satellites and things that astronauts have dropped on spacewalks. This junk is extremely dangerous. It orbits at more than 17,000 miles (28,000 kilometers per hour). It could crash into satellites, rockets, or even the *International Space Station (ISS)*.

satellites (SAT-uh-lites): spacecraft sent into orbit around Earth, the moon, or another celestial body

Hundreds of new satellites are being launched into space every year.

Safety in Space

In high school, Amber Yang developed a computer program to predict where space junk would orbit. This could warn astronauts if any pieces of junk get dangerously close to Earth.

The way we think about space has changed. When Jules Verne wrote about flying to the moon, people thought it was impossible. Airplanes didn't even exist! But times have changed. Buzz Aldrin and Neil Armstrong landed on the moon in 1969. Recently, U.S. astronaut Christina Koch spent 328 days in space. The company SpaceX can launch 60 or more satellites with each rocket.

These events would seem impossible to people who lived just a hundred years ago. So we should ask ourselves—what seems impossible to us?

Apollo 11 launched the first astronauts to land on the moon.

Probably the most surprising idea that might become a reality is a space elevator. Think of it like this: stretch a very strong cable from the ground to thousands of miles into space. An elevator would go up and down along the cable. Does it sound crazy? China hopes to build one within 30 years!

If that's amazing, then what other things haven't we thought of? What other incredible, astounding inventions does the future hold as we continue to imagine space?

A space elevator will likely be built in the next few decades.

NASA Posters

A creative team at the Jet Propulsion Laboratory (JPL), known as "The Studio," created the poster series, which is titled "Visions of the Future." Nine artists, designers, and illustrators were involved in designing the 14 posters.

Index

After-Reading Questions

1. What do you call the scientific study of outer space?

2. What different beliefs did some ancient societies have about the stars and planets?

3. What did Ptolemy believe about the relationship between Earth and the universe?

4. What two astronauts first landed on the moon?

5. How has our view of outer space changed over time?

Activity

Think about movies or stories that take place in outer space. What things do you think are impossible? What things do you think will come true? Write a paragraph or two about what you would like to do if you went into outer space.

About the Author

Mike Downs enjoys writing books for young readers. He especially loves writing about outer space. If he ever has a chance to ride in a rocket ship, he'll do it! Until then, he has to write from his desk at home.

www.rourkeeducationalmedia.com

PHOTO CREDITS: cover: ©ClaudioVentrella/ Getty Images; cover: ©jamesbenet/ Getty Images; cover, pages 3, 6, 10, 12, 14, 16, 18, 22, 26 28: ©LineTale/ Shutterstock.com; pages 4-5: ©MarcelC/ Getty Images; pages 4-6, 8-10, 12-16, 18-22, 24-26, 28, 30-31: ©kevron2001/ Getty Images; pages 6-7: ©FrankvandenBergh; pages 6-7: ©Tatyanash, ©kkraus/ Shutterstock.com; page 9: ©SiberianArt; pages 10-11: ©Pictures From History/Newscom; page 11: ©Anastazzo/ Getty Images; pages 12-13: ©Oleg Golovnev/ Shutterstock.com; page13: ©Prachaya Roekdeethaweesab/ Shutterstock.com; pages 14-15: ©Fine Art Images Heritage Images/Newscom; page 15: ©Wikimedia Commons/PD-US; pages 16-17: ©3000ad/ Shutterstock.com; pages 18-19: ©tsuneomp/ Shutterstock.com; page 19: ©Swill Klitch/ Shutterstock.com; pages 20-21: ©chainatp/ Getty Images; pages 22-23: ©aaronpastura/ Shutterstock.com; pages 24-25: ©Paul Fleet/ Shutterstock.com; page 25: ©dottedhippo/ Getty Images; pages 28-29: ©Wikimedia Commons/NASA/Pat Rawlings; page 30: ©NASA/JPL-Caltech

Edited by: Jennifer Doyle
Cover and interior design by: Alison Tracey

Library of Congress PCN Data

Imagining Space /
(Reaching for the Stars)
ISBN 978-1-73164-934-8 (hard cover)(alk. paper)
ISBN 978-1-73164-882-2 (soft cover)
ISBN 978-1-73164-986-7 (e-Book)
ISBN 978-1-73165-038-2 (ePub)
Library of Congress Control Number: 2021935271

Rourke Educational Media
Printed in the United States of America
01-1872111937